Chinese Jump Rope

▼

Sheree S. Marty

D1248115

 Sterling Publishing Co., Inc. New York

For my children,
Jessica and Jordan,
and
my mother,
Janet Thompson.

Library of Congress Cataloging-in-Publication Data

Marty, Sheree S.
    Chinese jump rope / by Sheree S. Marty.
        p.   cm.
    Includes index.
    ISBN 0-8069-0352-X
    1. Rope skipping—Juvenile literature.   2. Games—China—
Juvenile literature. [1. Rope skipping.   2. Games—China]   I. Title.
GV498.M37   1994
796.2—dc20   93-43812
                                                  CIP
                                                    AC

10   9 8 7 6 5 4 3 2 1

Published by Sterling Publishing Company, Inc.
387 Park Avenue South, New York, N.Y. 10016
© 1994 by Sheree S. Marty
Distributed in Canada by Sterling Publishing
℅ Canadian Manda Group, P.O. Box 920, Station U
Toronto, Ontario, Canada M8Z 5P9
Distributed in Great Britain and Europe by Cassell PLC
Villiers House, 41/47 Strand, London WC2N 5JE, England
Distributed in Australia by Capricorn Link (Australia) Pty Ltd.
P.O. Box 6651, Baulkham Hills, Business Centre, NSW 2153, Australia
Manufactured in the United States of America
All rights reserved

Sterling ISBN 0-8069-0352-X

Contents

PREFACE

Chinese jump rope found me as a child and once again through my profession as a physical educator. The game is funny like that, popping up from generation to generation, verbally passed from one to another like a folk tale. Many thanks to those whose shared games sparked the idea for this book, possibly preventing the eventual loss of the game to the ages. I am also forever indebted to those who believe in me. You know who you are. Thank you.

Sheree S. Marty
Palm Bay, Florida

1
Chinese Jump Rope

Chinese jump rope is a challenging game played by anyone anywhere. The simple rules test the skill and coordination of all players. An elastic rope is the only equipment needed for play. The game is easily learned and always fun. Chinese children first played Chinese jump rope in the seventh century. Rediscovered by English children in the 1960s, Chinese jump rope remains as popular as ever.

The Chinese Jump Rope

The rope used in Chinese jump rope is actually a long length of elastic. Special elastic ropes are available at local toy and department stores, but ropes are also easily constructed.

Constructing a Chinese Jump Rope

♦ **Method A** **Materials needed:** Scissors, measuring tape or ruler, ¼-inch (60 mm) elastic (available at fabric stores).

    SAFETY TIP: Ask permission from an adult before using scissors!

1. Measure a 72-inch (1.8 m) length of elastic.
2. Cut.
3. Knot the ends together.

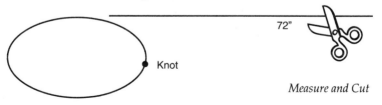

Knot

72"

Measure and Cut

♦ **Method B** **Materials needed:** Measuring tape or ruler, rubber bands (purchased by the bag).

SAFETY TIP: Rubber-band ropes can snap and sting a jumper's legs. To prevent "rubber-band snap," do not stretch the completed jump rope taut. Hold a rubber-band rope loosely.

1. Begin with two rubber bands.
2. Loop the two rubber bands together.
   - a. Place the top end of one rubber band over the bottom end of the second rubber band.
   - b. Pull the bottom end of the top rubber band under and through the bottom end of the second rubber band.
   - c. Pull tight. The rubber bands are looped.

| a. | b. | c. |
| "over" | "under and through" | "pull tight" |

Looping Rubber Bands

4. Loop additional rubber bands end to end until the rope measures 15 feet (4.5 m).
5. Knot the ends together.

Rubber Band Rope

Preparing for Play

Jump on any flat, even surface free of hazards such as rocks, glass, cracks, water, or traffic. Although Chinese jump rope requires at least three players, a single player can practice alone.

♦ **Practice Method A**

1. Draw two parallel chalk lines on the play surface (sidewalk, concrete, pavement).
2. Jump patterns using the chalk lines as a Chinese jump rope.

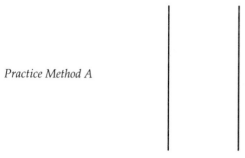

Practice Method A

♦ **Practice Method B**

1. Place two heavy chairs the length of one rope.
2. Anchor the rope under the front legs of both chairs and stretch it taut.
3. Practice jumping, substituting the chairs as enders.

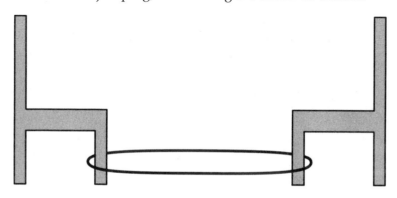

Practice Method B

SAFETY TIP: Allow plenty of jumping space indoors. Also, be certain both chairs are heavy enough to support the weight and movement of the jumper.

Warm-ups

Chinese jump rope is a vigorous activity and physically tough on jumping legs. Prepare the body for the game. Warm up with these simple exercises.

SAFETY TIP: Take a few moments for warm-ups to prevent muscular injury.

♦ **Full Body Stretch**
1. Stand tall.
2. Reach high over the head with straight arms.
3. Stretch!
4. Hold for ten seconds.
Arms, chest, and shoulders warm!

Full Body Stretch

♦ **Arm Circles**
1. Stand tall with arms straight at sides.
2. Circle straight arms forward ten circles.
3. Circle straight arms backwards ten circles.
Shoulders warm!

Arm Circles

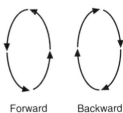

Forward   Backward

◆ Body Twists

1. Stand tall, arms straight out each side.
2. Twist side to side ten times.

Waist warm!

Body Twists

◆ Body Hang

1. Stand tall. Relax.
2. Slowly bend forward. Head and arms hang loose.
3. Hang twenty seconds.
4. Raise body slowly.

Lower back and hamstrings
(back thigh muscles) warm!

Body Hang

◆ Front Thigh Stretch

1. Stand tall. Balance the body by holding on to an object.
2. Bend one leg behind the body. The knee is bent. Hold the ankle with the free hand. Pull up slowly.
3. Stretch! Hold for ten seconds.
4. Repeat with opposite leg.

Quadriceps (front thigh muscles) warm!

Front Thigh Stretch

◆ Point and Flex
1. Stand tall. Lift one leg slightly.
2. Point the toe. Hold for ten seconds.
3. Flex the toe. (Bend toes toward body). Hold for ten seconds.
4. Repeat with the opposite foot.

Calf muscles (lower back leg muscles) warm!

Point and Flex

◆ Ankle Circles
1. Stand tall. Lift one leg slightly.
2. Circle one foot five times to the left.
3. Circle that foot five times to the right.
4. Repeat with the other foot.

Ankles warm!

Ankle Circles

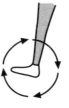
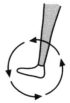

◆ Line Jump
1. Place the jump rope on the play surface.
2. Jump side to side back and forth over the rope fast.
3. Jump ten times.

Heart warm!

Line Jump

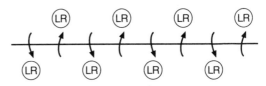

With the body warm and ready, it is time to jump feet first into the world of Chinese jump rope!

2
The Challenge

Chinese jump rope is no ordinary "rope skipping" game. *Enders* hold an elastic rope while a *jumper* jumps the rope in special ways. The challenge? To jump successfully!

The Game

The enders place the rope in *basic position* before any jumping begins.

Basic Position

Enders
1. Face each other.
2. Step inside the rope.
3. Place the rope around the ankles.
4. Step back until the rope is stretched tight.

Two parallel jumping lines, about 12 inches (30 cm) apart, are stretched between the enders. The jumper stands outside the rope, ready to play.

Rules

A jumper jumps until a mistake is made. A mistake is called a *miss*. A miss is made if a jumper makes a jumping mistake. For example, Sally jumps "out" of the ropes instead of "in." She misses.

"Miss" Illustration

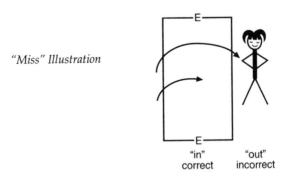

"in"   "out"
correct   incorrect

A miss is also made if a jumper touches the rope incorrectly. For example, Sally trips over the rope while jumping. She misses.

Incorrect "Touch"

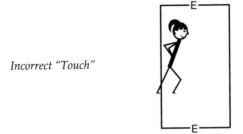

After a miss, the jumper trades positions with an ender. The jumper starts from the beginning of the game on the next turn.

"Try," "Savings," and "Pinkies"

The rope is raised from low to high in many games. Three special rules help a player jump raised ropes: "try," "savings," and "pinkies."

"Try": A jumper's first miss does not count. The jumper can try again. Jumpers can use only one "try" per rope level.

"Try" rule

Here's an example: Enders hold the rope at knee level. Sally, the jumper, tangles her foot in the rope, making a miss. She uses a "try" and tries again. Sally cannot use another "try" until the enders raise the ropes from the knees to the waist, the next jumping level.

"Savings": A jumper's second miss can be saved by the next player in line. The saving player must jump the miss two times correctly to save the jumper. The saved player continues jumping the game. If the saving player misses, all players must start from the beginning of the game on their next turn.

Here's an example: Sally jumps "in" in the ropes instead of "on" them, making a miss. She has already used a "try" at this level and cannot use another. Jane, the next player in line, volunteers to save Sally's jump. Jane jumps Sally's miss correctly two times. Sally continues jumping the game.

"Savings" Rule

If Jane does not save Sally's miss, Sally's turn is over. Jane, Sally, and all other players must start from the beginning of the game on their next turns.

"Pinkies": This is a great rule to use when the rope is raised too high for safe jumping. The jumper pulls the rope down with a pinkie finger and continues jumping without touching the rope with her feet. The right pinkie is used for a right jump. The left pinkie is used for a left jump. Do pinkies fast!

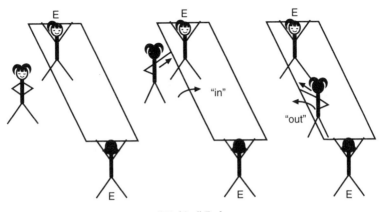

"Pinkies" Rule

Here's an example: The enders raise the rope above the head. Sally needs to jump "in," but the rope is too high. She pulls the rope down using her right pinkie finger and jumps "in" fast. The next jump is "out," moving left. Sally pulls the rope down using her left pinkie and quickly jumps "out." She continues jumping the game. If a miss is made, Sally can also use the "try" and "savings" rules.

Winning

The first player finished wins the game. Only one player wins and the game ends quickly. *There is another way.*

Cooperative Chinese jump rope is popular because players encourage each other to jump their best. All players are teammates. Each player must jump one game. The game is won after *all* players finish jumping successfully. Jumpers win by working together, *cooperating,* as a team. Everyone wins or no one wins.

Chinese jump rope is also played just for fun. The group does not play to win. This is okay!

3
Let's Jump!

Time to get active!

Start Positions

Before any jumping begins, the enders place the rope in a start position: the basic, cone, or diamond position.

The Basic Position

Every Chinese jump rope game begins with the rope held in the basic position. All other starting positions form from the basic position.

Basic Position

Enders
1. Face each other.
2. Step inside the rope.
3. Place the rope around the ankles.
4. Step back until the rope is stretched.

Two parallel jumping lines, about 12 inches (30 cm) apart, are stretched between the enders. The jumper stands outside the rope, ready to play.

Cone Position

The Cone Position

Enders
1. Place the rope in the basic position.
2. Ender 1: Keep the rope around both ankles.
3. Ender 2: Pull one foot outside the rope. The rope is now held around one ankle.

A cone shape is stretched between the enders. The jumper stands outside the rope, ready to play.

Diamond Position

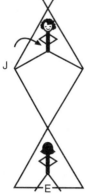

The Diamond Position

Enders
1. Place the rope in the basic position.
2. Relax! The jumper shapes the diamond.
Jumper
1. Face an ender.
2. Place one foot under the outside of the close rope. With the same foot, step over the far rope, carrying the close rope.
3. Step inside the rope with the other foot.
4. Form the diamond shape with both feet.

Jumping Patterns

A jumping pattern is a series of jumping steps. Simple words describe the simple steps.

"In": Jump inside the rope. Both feet land inside.

"On": Jump on top of the rope. The left foot lands on the left rope; the right foot lands on the right rope.

"Out": Jump outside the rope. Both feet land outside.

"Side out": Jump over the rope. Both feet land outside the rope on the same side.

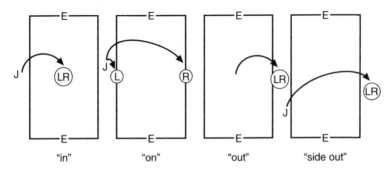

"in"   "on"   "out"   "side out"

"Straddle out": The left foot lands outside the left side of the rope. The right foot lands outside the right side of the rope. A straddle is formed.

"Side-by-side": A quick side-to-side jump. A "side-by-side" is as follows:

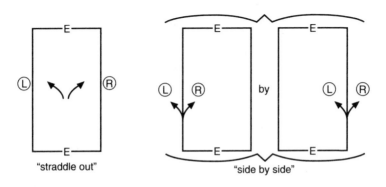

"straddle out"   "side by side"

Jumper

1. Both feet start "out" on the left side of ropes.
2. *Jump side:* The left foot lands outside the left rope. The right foot lands inside the rope.
3. *Quickly jump side again.* The left foot lands inside the rope. The right foot lands outside the right rope.

Jumpers call the jumping patterns out loud while jumping. "In, out, side-by-side . . ." Calling helps the jumper remember the pattern. (When a "side out" or "straddle out" is jumped, the jumper just calls "out.")

Basic and Cone-Jumping Patterns

These jumping patterns are jumped with the rope held in the basic or cone positions. The jumper faces an ender while jumping.

♦ **Pattern 1:**

in	straddle out	side-by-side	on	in	side out

♦ **Pattern 2:**

side	in	straddle out	side-by-side	in	on	side
out						out

♦ **Pattern 3:**

side	side	on	side	side	on	side
out	out		out	out		out

♦ **Pattern 4:**

side-by-side	in	straddle out	in	on	side
					out

Different jumping patterns are created by changing the step order. Try it!

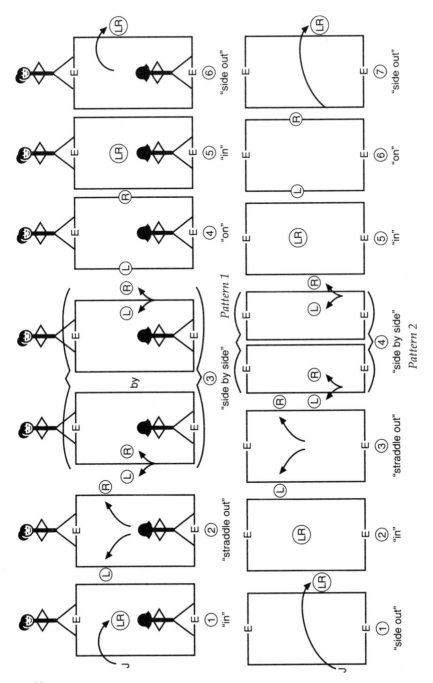

Pattern 1

Pattern 2

20

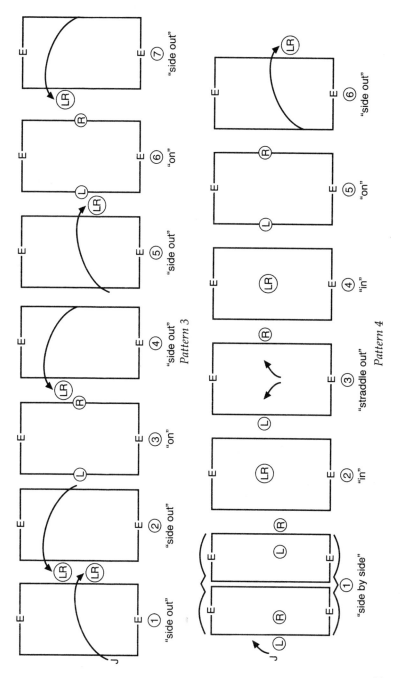

Pattern 3

① "side out"
② "side out"
③ "on"
④ "side out"
⑤ "side out"
⑥ "on"
⑦ "side out"

Pattern 4

① "side by side"
② "in"
③ "straddle out"
④ "in"
⑤ "on"
⑥ "side out"

21

Diamond Jumping Patterns

These jumping patterns are jumped in the diamond start position. The jumper faces an ender while jumping.

Circle-turns are jumped in the diamond patterns. Two half-turns equal one circle-turn. A circle-turn is as follows:

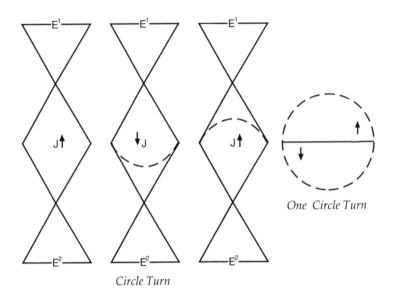

One Circle Turn

Circle Turn

Jumper
1. Face Ender 1.
2. Jump a half-turn. Face Ender 2.
3. Jump a half-turn. Face Ender 1.
4. One circle-turn is jumped.

♦ **Pattern 5:**
    in   five circle-turns   out

Pattern 5

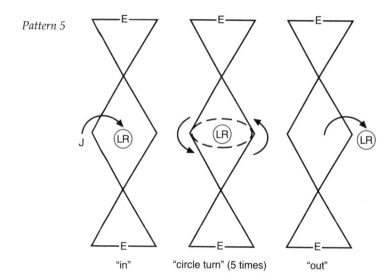

"in"   "circle turn" (5 times)   "out"

◆ **Pattern 6:**

in   spell name   out

Do one circle-turn for each letter of your name.

Try shaping a diamond in the cone start position. Jump patterns five and six. Good luck!

Pattern 6

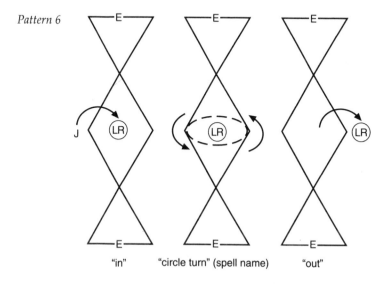

"in"   "circle turn" (spell name)   "out"

4
Jumping Sequences

A sequence is a series of jumping patterns jumped one after the other in a certain order. Sequences are beginning Chinese jump rope games.

Enders begin by holding the rope low. The rope is raised one level after each successfully jumped pattern. The jumper jumps the sequence at the new height and continues jumping raised ropes until a mistake is made.

Rope levels vary with each sequence but may include ankles, knees, ends of fingers with arms hanging straight down, hips, waist, underarms, shoulders, neck, ears, fist over head.

Sequences increase in difficulty as the rope reaches high levels. Remember, do not touch the ropes while jumping. Jumpers may use the "pinkies" rule for jumping high levels. Some sequences allow you to use your head, chin, or hands to motion the patterns instead of jumping high ropes. Advanced jumpers handstand or cartwheel "in" and "out" the high ropes. Safety is stressed for jumpers choosing this method.

Step-by-step instructions and illustrations describe each of the following sequences. Happy jumping!

Sequence One

♦ **Rope Start Position:** Basic
♦ **Number of Players:** 3
♦ **Player Positions**

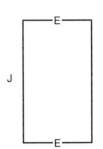

Basic Start Position

Enders (2): Hold the rope around the ankles in the basic position.

Jumper (1): Stand sidewards to the rope.

♦ **The Sequence**

1. **Jumper:** Jump Basic Pattern 1.

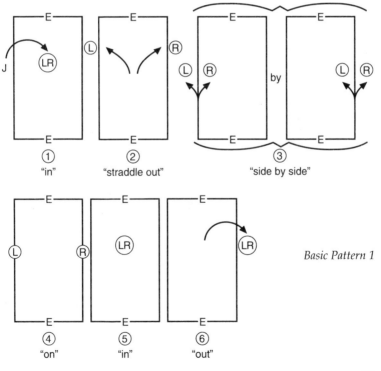

Basic Pattern 1

2. **Enders:** Raise the rope. Hold it at the knees.
   Jumper: Jump Basic Pattern 1.
3. **Enders:** Raise the rope. Hold it at waist level.
   Jumper: Jump Basic Pattern 1. (Careful! Do not touch the rope!)
4. **Enders:** Raise the rope. Hold it under your arms.
   Jumper: Step Basic Pattern 1. (Remember the "pinkie" rule!)
5. **Enders:** Raise the rope. Hold it around your neck.
   Jumper: Repeat Basic Pattern 1 using head and chin motions.
     1. Duck under ropes "in."
     2. Straddle out: Duck under rope right; duck under rope left.
     3. Side-by-side: From left, duck "in" rope; from "in," duck under to right.
     4. Duck "in." Touch chin "on" left rope; touch chin "on" right rope.
     5. Stay "in."
     6. Duck under rope to "side out."
6. **Enders:** Raise rope. Hold overhead with hands.
   Jumper: Repeat Basic Pattern 1 using hand motions. The jumper stands outside, facing the rope, while performing hand motions.
     1. Hands under rope "in."
     2. Hands under each side of the rope "straddle out."
     3. Hands under the rope, "side by side."
     4. Hands over rope, touching "on."
     5. Hands under rope "in."
     6. Hands under rope "out."

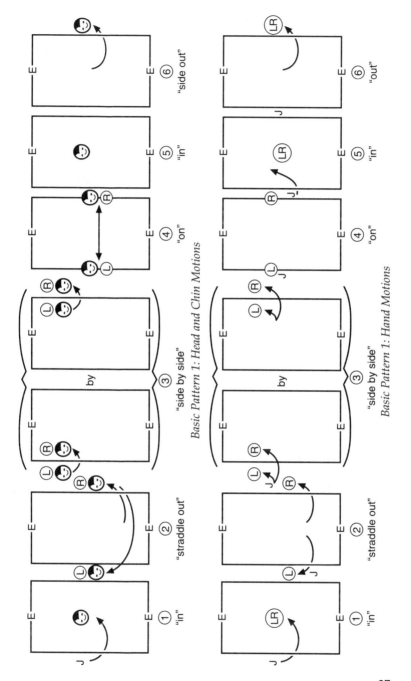

Basic Pattern 1: Head and Chin Motions

Basic Pattern 1: Hand Motions

27

Sequence Two

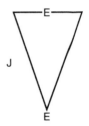

- ◆ **Rope Start Position:** Cone
- ◆ **Number of Players:** 3
- ◆ **Player Positions**

Cone Start Position

Enders (2): Hold rope around ankles in the cone position.
Jumper (1): Stand sidewards to the rope.

- ◆ **The Sequence**

  Part One: Ankles

  1. **Jumper:** Jump Cone Pattern 1.

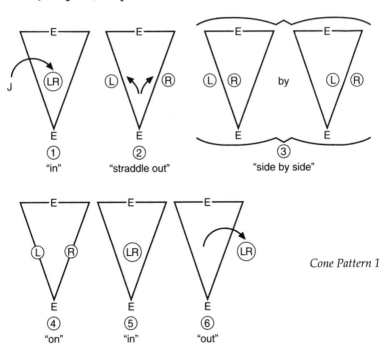

Cone Pattern 1

2. **Enders:** Continue holding the rope at ankle level in the cone position.

   Jumper: Jump Cone Pattern 2.

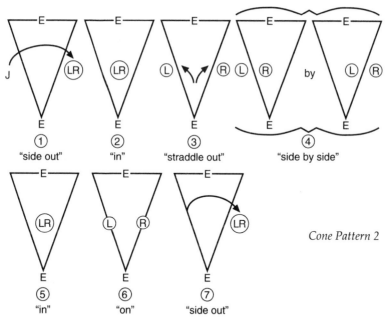

Cone Pattern 2

3. **Enders:** Continue holding the rope at ankle level in the cone position.
   Jumper: Jump Cone Pattern 3.

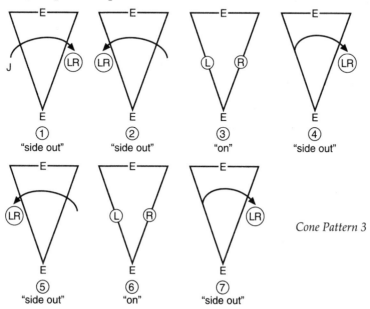

Cone Pattern 3

29

4. **Enders:** Continue holding rope at ankle level in the cone position.
   Jumper: Jump Cone Pattern 4.

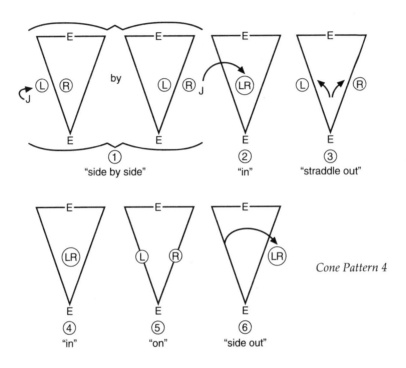

Cone Pattern 4

Part Two: Knees

1. **Enders:** Raise the ropes. Hold at knee level in the cone position.
   Jumper: Jump Cone Patterns 1–4.

Sequence Three

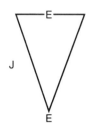

- ♦ **Rope Start Position:** Cone
- ♦ **Number of Players:** 3
- ♦ **Player Positions**

Cone Start Position

Enders (2): Hold the rope around the ankles in the cone position.

Jumper (1): Stand sidewards to the rope.

- ♦ **The Sequence**
    1. **Jumper:** Jump Cone Pattern 1.

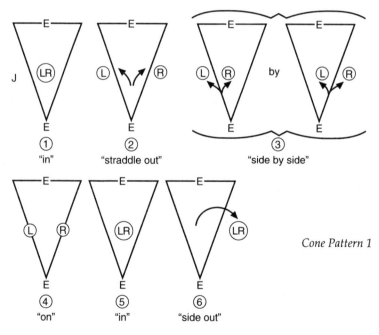

Cone Pattern 1

2. **Enders:** Continue holding the rope at ankle level in the cone position.

   Jumper: Step the rope into a diamond position. Jump Diamond Pattern 1. Jump out. The rope snaps back.

31

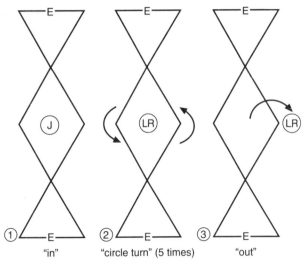

Diamond Pattern 1

"in" "circle turn" (5 times) "out"

3. **Enders:** Raise the rope. Hold the rope at knee level in the cone position.
   Jumper: Jump Cone Pattern 1.
4. **Enders:** Continue holding the rope at knee level in the cone position.
   Jumper: Step the rope into the diamond position. Jump Diamond Pattern 2. Jump out. The rope snaps back.

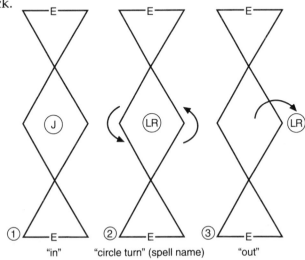

Diamond Pattern 2

"in" "circle turn" (spell name) "out"

Sequence Four

- **♦ Rope Start Position:** Basic
- **♦ Number of Players:** 3
- **♦ Player Positions**

Basic Start Position

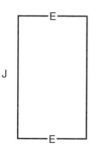

Enders (2): Hold the rope around the ankles in the basic position.

Jumper (1): Stand sidewards to the rope.

♦ The Sequence

1. **Jumper:** Jump Basic Pattern 1.

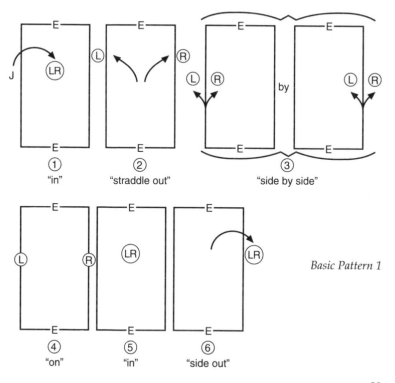

Basic Pattern 1

33

2. **Enders:** Continue holding the rope at ankle level in the basic position.
   Jumper: Step rope into the diamond position. Jump Diamond Pattern 1. Jump out. The rope snaps back straight.

Diamond Pattern 1

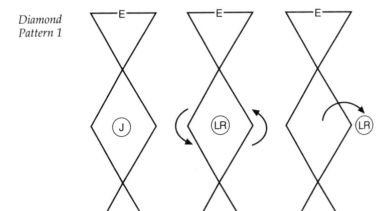

① "in"   ② "circle turn" (5 times)   ③ "out"

3. **Enders:** Raise the rope. Hold it at knee level.
   Jumper: Jump Basic Pattern 2.
4. **Enders:** Continue holding the rope at knee level in the basic position.
   Jumper: Step the rope into the diamond position. Jump Diamond Pattern 1. Jump out. The rope snaps back straight.
5. **Enders:** Raise the rope. Hold it at waist level.
   Jumper: Jump Basic Pattern 3.

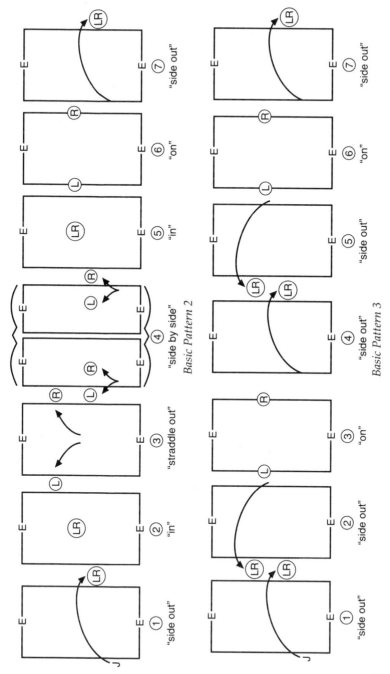

Basic Pattern 2

Basic Pattern 3

35

6. **Enders:** Continue holding the rope at knee level in the basic position.
   Jumper: Step the rope into the diamond position. Jump Diamond Pattern 1. Jump out. The rope snaps back straight.
7. **Enders:** Raise the rope. Hold it under your arms.
   Jumper: Step Basic Pattern 4. (Remember "pinkies"!)

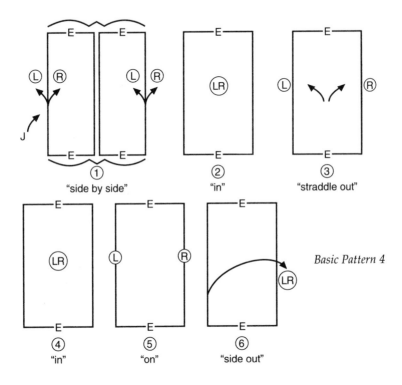

① "side by side"   ② "in"   ③ "straddle out"

④ "in"   ⑤ "on"   ⑥ "side out"

Basic Pattern 4

8. **Enders:** Continue holding the rope under your arms in the basic position.
   Jumper: Step the rope into the diamond position. Jump Diamond Pattern 1. Jump out. The rope snaps back straight.

Sequence Five

- ◆ **Rope Start Position:** Basic
- ◆ **Number of Players:** 3
- ◆ **Player Positions**

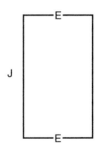

Basic Start Position

Enders (2): Hold rope around ankles in basic position.
Jumper (1): Stand sidewards to rope.

- ◆ **The Sequence**
    1. **Jumper:** Jump Basic Pattern 3.

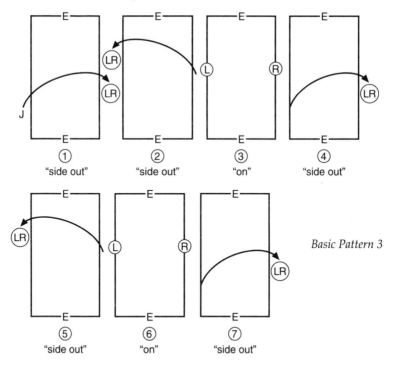

Basic Pattern 3

2. **Enders:** Continue holding the rope at ankle level in the basic position.

Jumper: Step the rope into the diamond position. Jump Diamond Pattern 2. Jump out. The rope snaps back straight.

Diamond Pattern 2

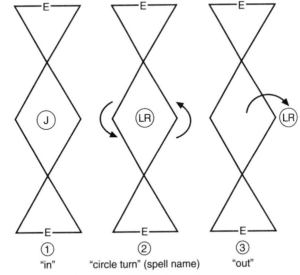

① "in"   ② "circle turn" (spell name)   ③ "out"

3. **Enders:** Raise the rope. Hold it at the knees.
   Jumper: Jump Basic Pattern 3.
4. **Enders:** Continue holding the rope around the knees in the basic position.
   Jumper: Step the rope into the diamond position. Jump Diamond Pattern 2. Jump out. The rope snaps back
5. **Enders:** Raise the rope. Hold it at the waist.
   Jumper: Jump Basic Pattern 3. (Careful! Do not touch the ropes!)
6. **Enders:** Continue holding the rope around your waist in the basic position.
   Jumper: Step the rope into the diamond position. Jump Diamond Pattern 2. Jump out. The rope snaps back.
7. **Enders:** Raise the rope. Hold it under your arms.
   Jumper: Step Basic Pattern 3. (Remember "pinkies"!)
8. **Enders:** Continue holding the rope under your arms in the basic position.

Jumper: Step the rope into the diamond position. Jump Diamond Pattern 2. Jump out. The rope snaps back.

9. **Enders:** Raise the rope. Hold it around the back of your neck.

    Jumper: Repeat Basic Pattern 3 using head and chin motions.

    1. Duck under the rope "side out."
    2. Repeat "side out" to the opposite side.
    3. Duck "in." Touch chin "on" rope left; touch chin "on" rope right.
    4. "Side out": Repeat #1.
    5. "Side out": Repeat #2.
    6. "On": Repeat #3.
    7. Duck under and "side out."

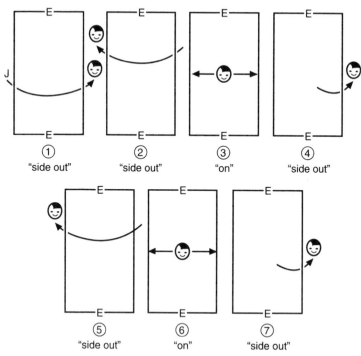

Basic Pattern 3: Head and Chin Motions

10. **Enders:** Continue holding the rope around the back of your neck in the basic position.

Jumper: Shape a diamond in the rope with your hands. The jumper stands outside facing the rope while performing Diamond Pattern 2 using hand motions.

1. Shape a diamond in the rope with your hands.
2. Circle-turn, spelling your name.
3. Hands under rope and out.

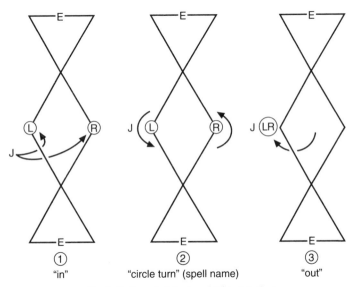

Basic Pattern 3: Head and Chin Motions

Sequence Six

PART ONE
- ◆ **Rope Start Position:** Basic
- ◆ **Number of Players:** 3
- ◆ **Player Positions**

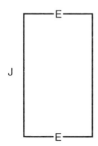

Basic Start Position

Enders (2): Hold the rope in the basic position.

Jumper (1): Stand sidewards to the rope.

◆ **The Sequence**
1. **Jumper:** Jump Basic Pattern 1, 2, 3, or 4. (See pages 42–43.)
2. **Enders:** Raise the rope. Hold it at knee level.
   Jumper: Repeat jumping the selected jumping pattern.
3. **Enders:** Raise the rope. Hold it at waist level.
   Jumper: Repeat jumping the selected jumping pattern. (Careful! Do not touch the rope!)
4. **Enders:** Raise the rope. Hold it under your arms.
   Jumper: Step the selected jumping pattern.
5. **Enders:** Raise the rope. Hold it around the back of your neck.
   Jumper: Repeat the selected jumping pattern using head and chin motions. (See pages 44–45.)

Head and chin motions

◆ **Pattern 1**
1. **"In":** Duck under the rope "in."
2. **"Straddle out":** duck under the rope right; duck under the rope left.
3. **"Side-by-side":** From the left, duck "in." From "in," duck right.
4. **"On":** Duck "in." Touch the chin left; touch it right.
5. **"In":** Stay "in."
6. **"Side out":** Duck under the rope "side out."

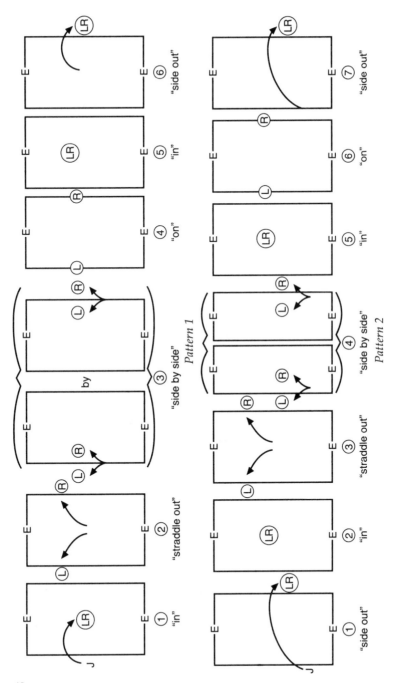

42

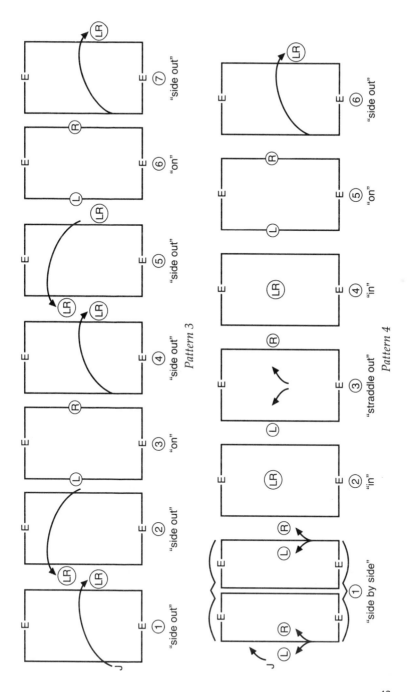

43

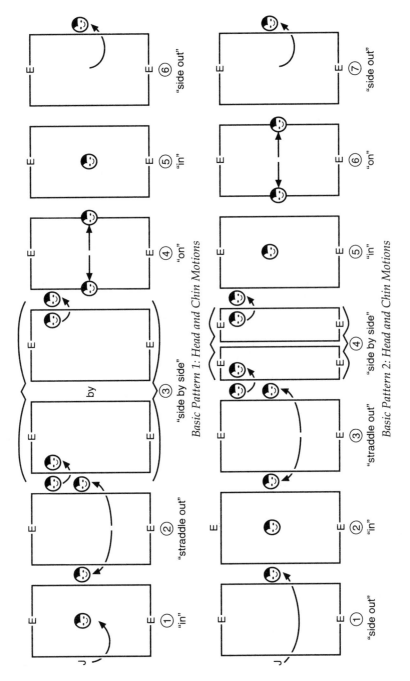

Basic Pattern 1: Head and Chin Motions

① "in" ② "straddle out" ③ "side by side" ④ "on" ⑤ "in" ⑥ "side out"

Basic Pattern 2: Head and Chin Motions

① "side out" ② "in" ③ "straddle out" ④ "side by side" ⑤ "in" ⑥ "on" ⑦ "side out"

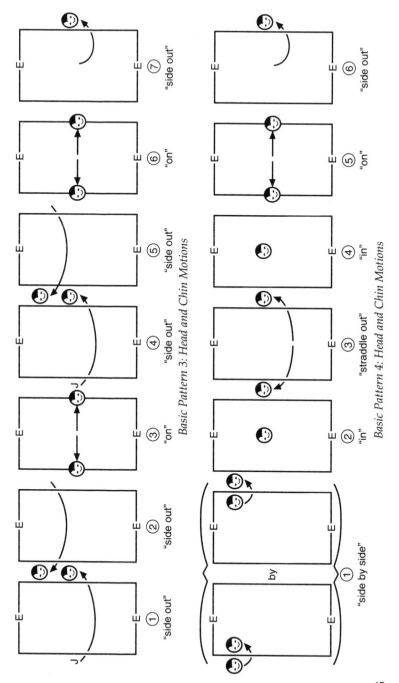

Basic Pattern 3: Head and Chin Motions

Basic Pattern 4: Head and Chin Motions

45

◆ Pattern 2

1. **"Side out"**: Duck under the rope "side out."
2. **"In"**: Duck "in."
3. **"Straddle out"**: Duck under the rope right; duck under the rope left.
4. **"Side-by-side"**: Duck "in"; duck "out."
5. **"In"**: Duck "in."
6. **"On"**: Touch the chin left; touch the chin right.
7. **"Side out"**: Duck under the rope "side out."

◆ Pattern 3

1. **"Side out"**: Duck under the rope "side out."
2. **"Side out"**: Repeat #1 to the opposite side.
3. **"On"**: Touch chin left; touch chin right.
4. **"Side out"**: Repeat #1.
5. **"Side out"**: Repeat #2.
6. **"On"**: Repeat #3.
7. **"Side out"**: Repeat #1.

◆ Pattern 4

1. **"Side-by-side"**: Duck "in"; duck "out."
2. **"In"**: Duck "in."
3. **"Straddle out"**: Duck under right; duck under left.
4. **"In"**: Duck "in."
5. **"On"**: Touch chin left; touch chin right.
6. **"Side out"**: Duck under rope "side out."

Enders: Raise the rope. Hold it overhead with your hands.

Jumper: Repeat the selected jumping pattern using your hand motions. (See pages 47–48.)

Hand motions
◆ Pattern 1

1. **"In"**: Hands under the rope "in."
2. **"Straddle out"**: Hands under the rope side to "straddle out."
3. **"Side-by-side"**: Hands under the rope "side by side."
4. **"On"**: Hands over the rope "on."
5. **"In"**: Hands over the rope to "in."
6. **"Side out"**: Hands under the rope "side out."

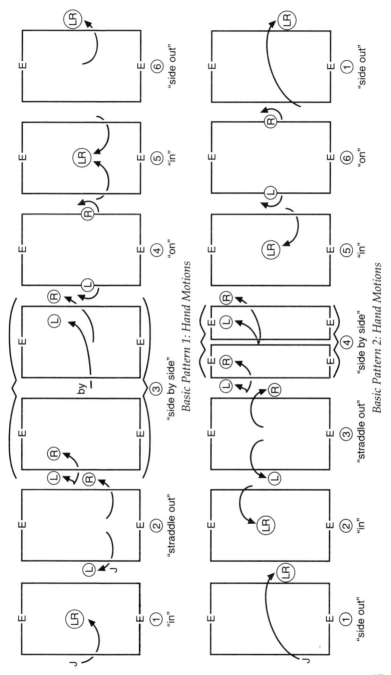

Basic Pattern 1: Hand Motions

Basic Pattern 2: Hand Motions

47

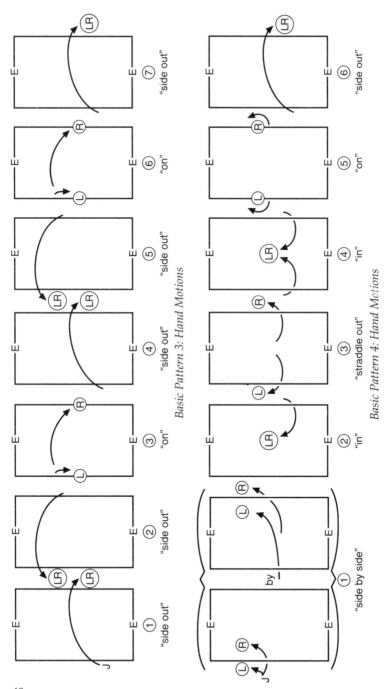

Basic Pattern 3: Hand Motions

Basic Pattern 4: Hand Motions

◆ Pattern 2
1. **"Side out"**: Hands over the rope "side out."
2. **"In"**: Hands over the rope "in."
3. **"Straddle out"**: Hands over the rope to "straddle out."
4. **"Side-by-side"**: Hands under "side by side."
5. **"In"**: Hands under the rope "in."
6. **"On"**: Hands over the rope "on."
7. **"Side out"**: Hands over the rope "side out."

◆ Pattern 3
1. **"Side out"**: Hands over the rope "side out."
2. **"Side out"**: Repeat #1.
3. **"On"**: Hands over the rope "on."
4. **"Side out"**: Hands over the rope "side out."
5. **"Side out"**: Repeat #4.
6. **"On"**: Repeat #3.
7. **"Side out"**: Repeat #4.

◆ Pattern 4
1. **"Side-by-side"**: Hands under the rope "side by side."
2. **"In"**: Hands under "in."
3. **"Straddle out"**: Hands under the rope sides to "straddle out."
4. **"In"**: Hands under "in."
5. **"On"**: Hands over "on."
6. **"Side out"**: Hands over "side out."

PART TWO
- ◆ **Rope Start Position:** Cone
- ◆ **Number of Players:** 3
- ◆ **Player Positions**

Cone Start Position

Enders (2): Lower the rope around the ankles to the cone position.

Jumper (1): Stand sidewards to the rope.
1. **Jumper:** Jump Cone Pattern 1, 2, 3, or 4. (See pages 50–51.)

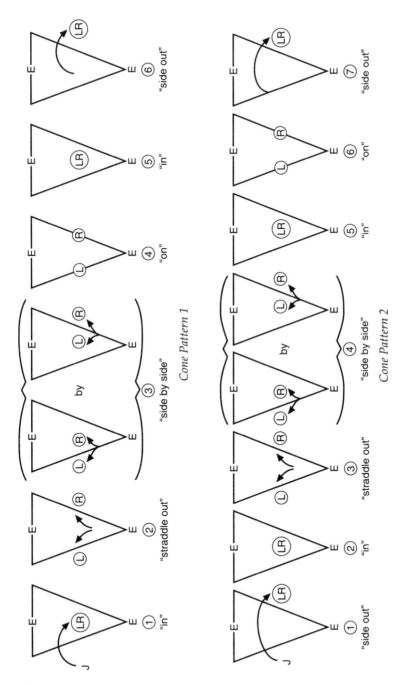

Cone Pattern 1

Cone Pattern 2

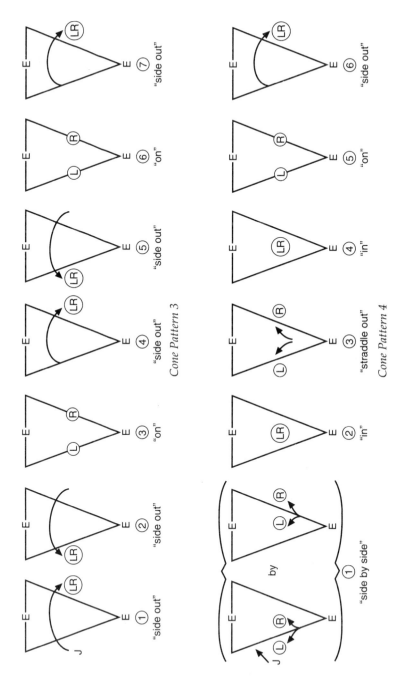

Cone Pattern 3

① "side out"

② "side out"

③ "on"

④ "side out"

⑤ "side out"

⑥ "on"

⑦ "side out"

Cone Pattern 4

① "side by side"

by

② "in"

③ "straddle out"

④ "in"

⑤ "on"

⑥ "side out"

2. **Enders:** Raise the rope to knee level in the cone position.

Jumper: Repeat jumping the selected jumping pattern.

PART THREE
♦ **Rope Start Position:** Basic
♦ **Number of Players:** 3
♦ **Player Positions**

Basic Start Position

Enders (2): Lower the rope around the ankles to the basic position.

Jumper (1): Stand sidewards to the rope.

1. **Jumper:** Step rope into the diamond position. Jump Diamond Pattern 1 or 2.

2. **Enders:** Raise the rope. Hold it at knee level.

Jumper: Step the rope into the diamond position. Repeat jumping the selected diamond jumping pattern.

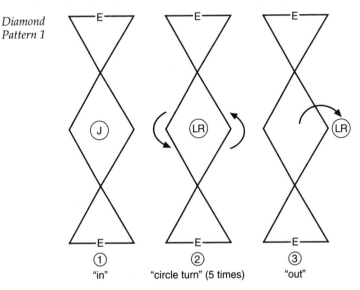

Diamond Pattern 1

① "in"   ② "circle turn" (5 times)   ③ "out"

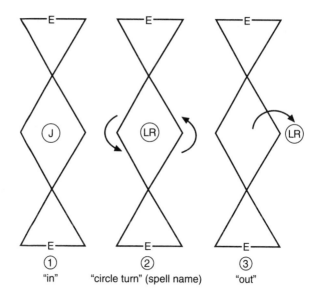

① "in" ② "circle turn" (spell name) ③ "out"

3. **Enders:** Raise the rope. Hold it at waist level.
    Jumper: Step the rope into the diamond position. Repeat jumping the selected diamond pattern.
4. **Enders:** Raise the rope. Hold it under your arms.
    Jumper: Step the rope into the diamond position. Repeat jumping the selected diamond jumping pattern.
5. **Enders:** Raise the rope. Hold it around the back of your neck.
    Jumper: Shape the diamond position in the rope with your hands. The jumper stands outside facing the rope while performing the selected diamond pattern with hand motions.

Hand motions

♦ **Diamond Pattern 1**

1. Shape a diamond in the rope with your hands.
2. Circle-turn five times.
3. Hands under the rope and "out."

♦ **Diamond Pattern 2**

1. Shape a diamond in the rope with your hands.
2. Circle-turn, spelling your name.
3. Hands under the rope and "out."

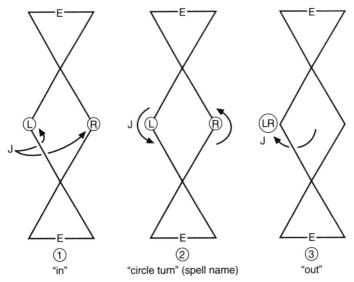

Basic Pattern 1: Head and Chin Motions

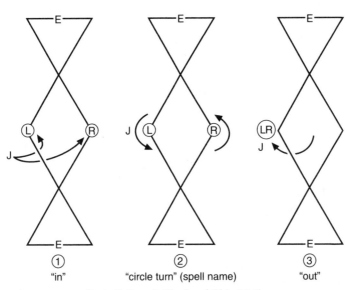

Basic Pattern 2: Head and Chin Motions

5
Favorite Games

A Chinese jump rope game is created by adding an *object* to a sequence. The object of a game is its purpose. What goals are the players aiming for in the game? For example, jumping over and out of the ropes at raised levels without a trip is the object of the Chinese jump rope game *Bunny Hops*. Objects differ with each game.

Favorite Chinese jump rope games are described and detailed in this chapter. Each game offers a unique challenge to the jumper. Ready? Set? Go!

Ordinaries and Opposites

- **Object:** To jump the pattern without a mistake.
- **Rope Start Position:** Basic
- **Number of Players:** 3
- **Player Positions**

Basic Start Position

Enders (2): Hold the rope around the ankles in the basic position.

Jumper (1): Stand facing the rope.

The Game

- **Action One:** Ordinaries

Jumper: Jump the "ordinaries" pattern.
1. Jump "in." Call "tinker in."
2. Jump "over out." Call "tinker over out."

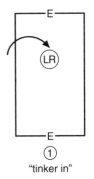

①
"tinker in"

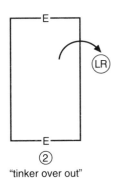

②
"tinker over out"

"Ordinaries" Pattern

- **Action Two:** Opposites

Jumper: Jump the "opposites" pattern.
1. Jump "over." Call "tinker over."
2. Jump "in." Call "tinker in."
3. Jump "out." Call "tinker out."

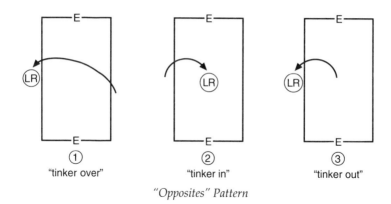

①	②	③
"tinker over"	"tinker in"	"tinker out"

"Opposites" Pattern

♦ **Action Three**

   Enders: Raise the rope to knee level.

   Jumper: Jump the "ordinaries" and "opposites" patterns.

♦ **Action Four**

   Enders: Raise the rope to hip level.

   Jumper: Jump the "ordinaries" and "opposites" patterns.

American Ropes

- **Object:** To manipulate the rope without a miss, using feet, chin, and head motions.
- **Rope Start Position:** Basic
- **Number of Players:** 3
- **Player Positions**

Basic Start Position

Enders (2): Hold the rope around the ankles in the basic position.

Jumper (1): Stand sidewards to the rope.

The Game

- **Action One**

    Jumper: Step inside the rope using the foot closest to the rope; step out.

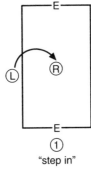

① "step in"

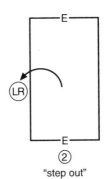

② "step out"

- **Action Two**

    Jumper: Slide the foot under the close rope. Lift and carry the close rope over the far rope, touching the jumping surface (ground, concrete) with the toe.

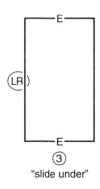

③
"slide under"

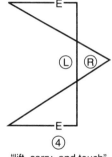

④
"lift, carry, and touch"

◆ Action Three

Jumper: Step the close rope back. Repeat action two: lift, carry, and touch ten times with the close foot.

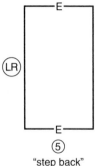

⑤
"step back"

◆ Action Four

Jumper: Change sides. Repeat actions one and two with the new close foot ten times.

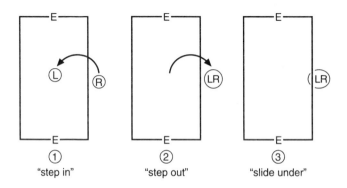

①	②	③
"step in"	"step out"	"slide under"

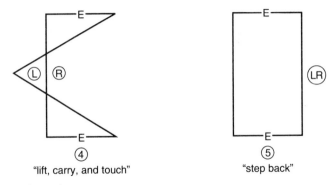

④
"lift, carry, and touch"

⑤
"step back"

◆ Action Five

Jumper: Jump inside the rope with both feet; jump out. Repeat ten times.

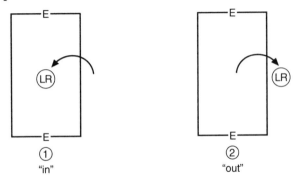

①
"in"

②
"out"

◆ Action Six

Jumper: Slide both feet under the close rope. Jump and carry the close rope over the far rope. Land on the jumping surface with both feet.

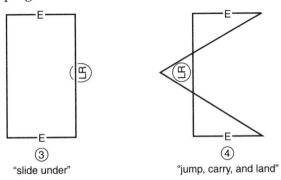

③
"slide under"

④
"jump, carry, and land"

♦ Action Seven

Jumper: Jumping backwards, jump the rope back. Repeat action six: jump, carry, and land ten times.

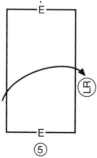

⑤
"jump rope back"

♦ Action Eight

Enders: Raise the rope to knee level.
Jumper: Repeat actions one through seven.

♦ Action Nine

Enders: Raise the rope to waist level.
Jumper: Repeat actions one through seven.

♦ Action Ten

Enders: Raise the rope to neck level.
Jumper: Face the rope. Repeat actions one through three using chin motions.

1. Chin "in" the rope; chin "out" of the rope.
2. Chin under the rope. Lift the close rope over the far rope.
3. Carry the rope back. The rope snaps back straight. Repeat ten times.

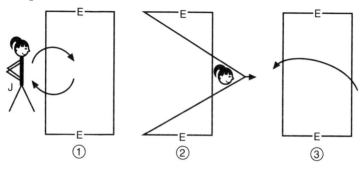

♦ Action Eleven

Enders: The rope remains at neck level.

Jumper: Face the rope. Repeat actions four through six using head motions.

Head Motions

1. Duck under the rope; duck "out" the rope. Repeat ten times.
2. Place the rope on top of your head. Lift the rope with your head and carry the rope. Touch your chin over the far rope.

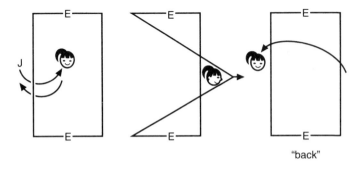

"back"

Head motions

1. Chin "in" the rope; chin "out" the rope.

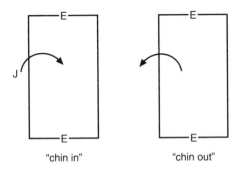

"chin in"   "chin out"

Head motions

1. Slide your head under the rope.
2. Lift, carry, and touch over the opposite rope ten times.

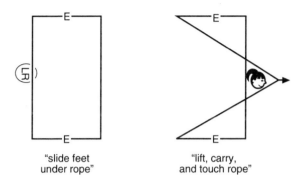

"slide feet
under rope"

"lift, carry,
and touch rope"

Peter Pansies

♦ **Object:** To jump fast at raised levels without a miss.
♦ **Rope Start Position:** Basic
♦ **Number of Players:** 3
♦ **Player Positions**

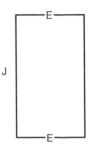

Basic Position   J

Enders (2): Hold the rope around the ankles in the basic
    position.
Jumper (1): Stand sidewards to the rope.

The Game

♦ **Action One**

Jumper: Jump the "Peter Pansies" pattern fast!
1. Jump "side."
2. Slide the inside foot to the side, stretching the far rope.
3. Step the outside foot "in."
4. Jump "side." The rope snaps straight.
5. Slide the inside foot to the side, stretching far rope.
6. Step the outside foot "in."
7. Jump "side." The rope snaps straight.

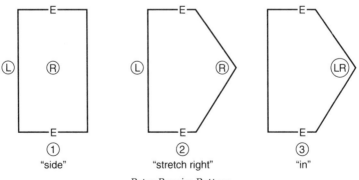

Peter Pansies Pattern

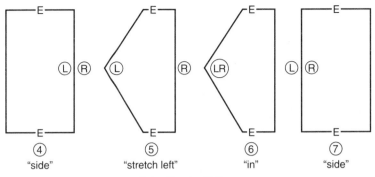

Peter Pansies Pattern

♦ **Action Two**

   Enders: Continue holding the rope at ankle level.

   Jumper: Jump the "Peter Pansies" pattern four more times. Remember, jump fast!

♦ **Action Three**

   Enders: Raise the rope to knee level.

   Jumper: Jump five fast "Peter Pansies."

♦ **Action Four**

   Enders: Raise the rope to waist level.

   Jumper: Jump five fast "Peter Pansies."

Bunny Hops

- **Object:** To jump over and out of the rope at raised levels without a miss.
- **Rope Start Position:** Basic
- **Number of Players:** 3
- **Player Positions**

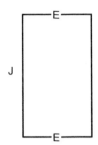

Basic Position

Enders (2): Hold the rope around the ankles in the basic
  position.
Jumper (1): Stand facing the rope.

The Game

- **Action One**

  Jumper: Slide both feet under the close rope. Jump and carry the close rope over the far rope.

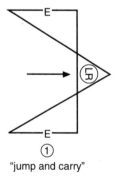

①
"jump and carry"

- **Action Two**

  Jumper: Jump "out." The rope snaps back straight. The jumper has jumped one bunny-hop.

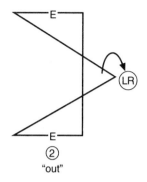

"out"

♦ Action Three

Jumper: Face the rope. Repeat actions one and two, bunny-hopping in a new direction. Jump five bunny-hops.

♦ Action Four

Enders: Raise the rope to knee level.

Jumper: Repeat actions one through three.

Poison Ivy I

♦ **Object:** To jump the patterns without touching the slanted ropes.
♦ **Rope Start Position:** Slanted Basic
♦ **Number of Players:** 3
♦ **Player Positions**

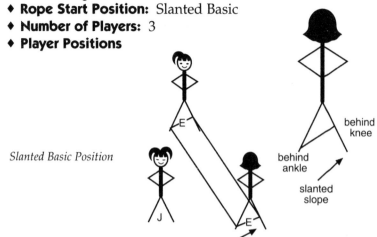

Slanted Basic Position

Enders (2): Hold the ropes slanted. Each ender holds the left side of the rope around the left ankle. The right side of the rope is held behind the right knee.

Jumper (1): Stand sidewards to the rope. Prepare to jump right.

The Game

♦ **Action One**

Jumper: Jump the "Poison Ivy" pattern without touching the rope with your feet, except when jumping "on": "In, on, side-by-side, in, on, stretch out, side out."

♦ **Action Two**

Enders: Reverse the slant of the rope. Each ender holds the right side of the rope around the right ankle. The left side of the rope is held behind the left knee.

Jumper: Prepare to jump left. Repeat the jumping of the "Poison Ivy" pattern.

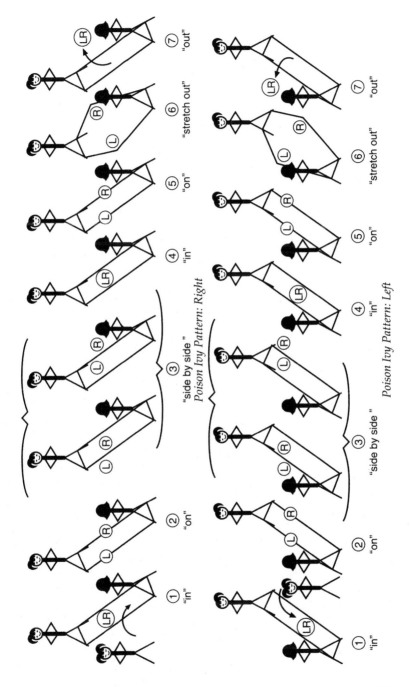

Poison Ivy Pattern: Right

① "in" ② "on" ③ "side by side" ④ "in" ⑤ "on" ⑥ "stretch out" ⑦ "out"

Poison Ivy Pattern: Left

① "in" ② "on" ③ "side by side" ④ "in" ⑤ "on" ⑥ "stretch out" ⑦ "out"

Poison Ivy II

♦ **Object:** To jump the patterns without touching the slanted ropes.
♦ **Rope Start Position:** Slanted Basic.
♦ **Number of Players:** 3
♦ **Player Positions**

Slanted Basic Position

Enders (2): Hold the rope slanted. Each ender holds the left side of the rope around the left ankle. The right side of the rope is held behind the right knee.

Jumper (1): Stand sidewards to the rope. Prepare to jump right.

The Game

♦ **Action One:**

Jumper: Face the rope. Jump "in" over the low rope. Jump "out" over the high rope. Remember, no touching!

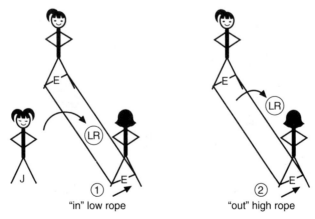

"in" low rope   "out" high rope

70

♦ **Action Two:**

Jumper: Stand with back to the rope. Jump backwards, over the high rope, "in." Jump backwards, over the low rope, "out."

① "in" high rope: backwards

② "out" low rope: backwards

♦ **Action Three:**

Jumper: Repeat actions one and two five times.

♦ **Action Four:**

Enders: Keep the rope in slanted basic.

Jumper: Repeat actions one and two using hand motions only.

Hand motions
1. Hands over the low rope "in."
2. Hands over the high rope "out."

Hand motions
1. Hands back over the high rope "in."
2. Hands back over the low rope "out."

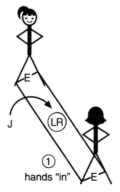

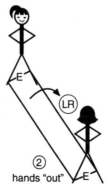

① hands "in"

② hands "out"

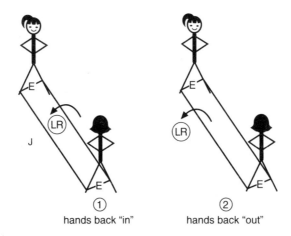

① hands back "in"   ② hands back "out"

◆ Action Five:

Enders: Keep the rope in slanted basic.

Jumper: Repeat actions one and two touching the hands and feet to the ground upon landing.

① hands and feet "in"   ② hands and feet "out"

① hands and feet "in"   ② hands and feet "out"

♦ Action Six:

Enders: Keep the rope in slanted basic.

Jumper: Jump forward over both lengths of rope. Jump backwards over both lengths of rope. Touch your hands and feet to the ground upon landing. Repeat five times.

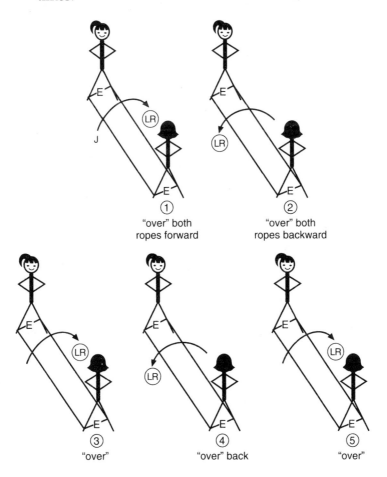

① "over" both ropes forward

② "over" both ropes backward

③ "over"

④ "over" back

⑤ "over"

Hong Kong Jump

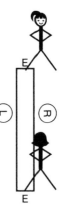

- ◆ **Object:** To escape the twist successfully.
- ◆ **Rope Start Position:** Basic
- ◆ **Number of Players:** 3
- ◆ **Player Positions**

Modified Basic Position

Enders (2): Hold the rope around one ankle in the basic position.

Jumper (1): Stand facing the rope.

The Game

- ◆ **Action One**

  Jumper: Slide one foot under the rope. Step one foot over the rope.

- ◆ **Action Two**

  Jumper: Wrap both ankles in the rope by jumping, twisting, and turning.

- ◆ **Action Three**

  Jumper: Escape! Unravel the ropes from your ankles by jumping, twisting, and turning in the opposite direction.

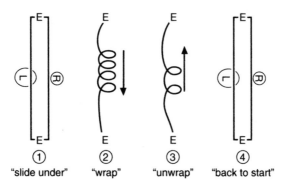

Sentra

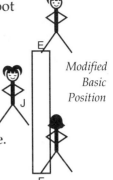

Modified Basic Position

- **Object**: To manipulate the rope using foot and hand motions.
- **Rope Start Position**: Modified Basic
- **Number of Players**: 3
- **Player Positions**

  Enders (2): Hold the rope around one ankle in the basic position.

  Jumper (1): Stand sidewards to the rope.

The Game

- **Action One**

  Jumper: Jump the "Sentra" pattern. "Side out, side out, on, side out."

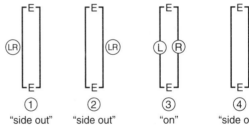

"Sentra" Pattern

① "side out" ② "side out" ③ "on" ④ "side out"

- **Action Two**

  Enders: Raise the rope and hold it at neck level.

  Jumper: Perform the following pattern using hand motions:

  1. Right hand "in" over rope; left hand "in" under rope.
  2. Reverse hands. Left hand "in" over rope; right hand "in" under rope.
  3. Hold rope with hands. Cross back and forth, spelling S-O-S.

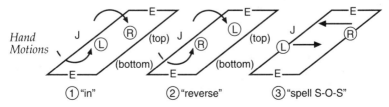

Hand Motions

① "in" ② "reverse" ③ "spell S-O-S"

X's

♦ **Object:** To manipulate the raised rope without a miss.
♦ **Rope Start Position:** Modified Basic
♦ **Number of Players:** 3
♦ **Player Positions**

Modified Basic Position

Enders (2): Using hands, hold the rope in the basic position. One ender crosses the rope once, forming an X. Both enders place the rope around the ankles, keeping the X formation.

Jumper (1): Face the X from the side.

The Game

♦ **Action One:**
Jumper:
1. Jump into the X with the right foot on one side of the X and the left foot on the opposite side of the X.
2. Jump out.

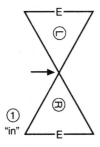
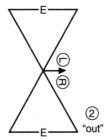

♦ **Action Two**
Jumper: Face the opposite direction. Repeat action one. This completes one X pattern.

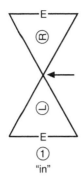
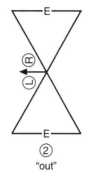

①
"in"

②
"out"

♦ Action Three
Jumper: Jump five X patterns.

♦ Action Four
Enders: Raise the rope to knee level.
Jumper: Jump five X's.

♦ Action Five
Enders: Raise the rope to hip level.
Jumper: Jump five X's.

♦ Action Six
Enders: Raise the ropes under the armpits.
Jumper: Perform five X's using hand motions.

1. Left hand "in" left side of X; right hand "in" right side of X.
2. Left and right hands reach "over" the rope to "out."
3. The jumper changes position to the opposite side of the rope. Repeat "in" and "out."
4. One X is complete. Repeat until five X's are completed.

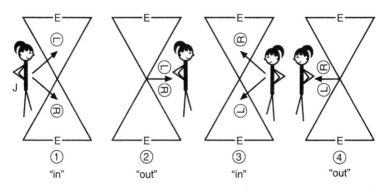

①
"in"

②
"out"

③
"in"

④
"out"

Abraham

- ◆ **Object:** To escape the twist successfully.
- ◆ **Rope Start Position:** Modified Cone
- ◆ **Number of Players:** 5
- ◆ **Player Positions**

Modified Cone

> **Enders (4):** Ender 1 holds the rope around one ankle. Enders 2, 3, and 4 step inside the rope and shape the cone.
>
> **Jumper (1):** The jumper stands to the side.

The Game

- ◆ **Action One**

Jumper:

1. Jump over the rope.
2. The jumper steps one foot "in" and twists the rope around one ankle several times.
3. Jump "out" of the twist and "over" to the opposite side.

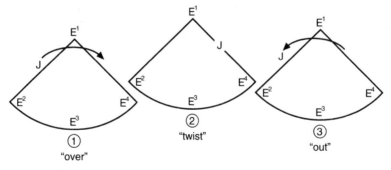

- ◆ **Action Two**

Jumper: Shape the diamond in the rope.

1. Twist the rope around one ankle.

2. Unwind the twist and step "out." The rope snaps back straight.

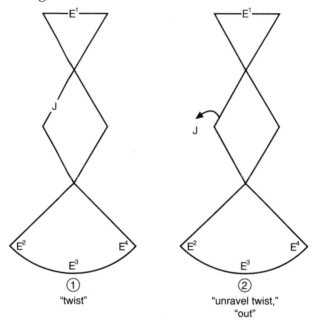

① "twist"

② "unravel twist," "out"

♦ **Action Three**

Enders: Ender 1 keeps the rope at ankle level. Enders 2, 3, and 4 raise the rope around the back of their necks, slanting the cone.

Jumpers (2): Two jumpers are needed for action three. Jumpers step inside the rope.

1. Jumper 1 twists jumper 2 inside the rope.
2. Jumper 1 steps out. Jumper 2 has three minutes to escape the twist.

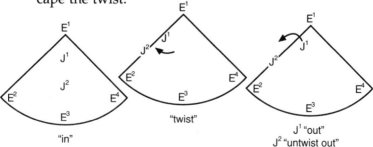

"in"

"twist"

J^1 "out"
J^2 "untwist out"

Partner Jump

♦ **Object:** To perform patterns in unison with a partner, using *two* lengths of rope.
♦ **Number of Players:** 4
♦ **Rope Start Position:** Basic
♦ **Player Positions**

Basic Position

Enders (2): Hold two lengths of rope around the ankles in the basic position.

Jumper (2): Jump "Partners" together.

The Game

♦ **Action One**

Jumper: Jump "Partners" together.
1. Jump "on" both lengths of rope.
2. Jump "out" both lengths of rope.
3. Jump "in" both lengths of rope.
4. Jump "out" both lengths of rope.

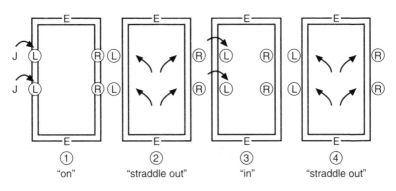

◆ Action Two

Jumper: One jumper shapes a double diamond in the ropes.

1. Partner joins partner "in" the diamond.
2. The jumpers "spin" three times.
3. The jumpers jump "out" of the ropes, then "on" as the ropes snap back straight.

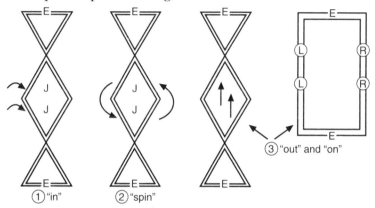

◆ Action Three

Enders: Raise ropes to calves.

Jumpers: Jump actions one and two at this level.

◆ Action Four

Enders: Raise ropes to your knees.

Jumpers: Jump actions one and two.

Advanced jumpers: Jump with your eyes closed.

◆ Action Five

Enders: Raise ropes to waist.

Jumpers: Jump actions one and two.

◆ Action Six

Enders: Raise ropes under armpits.

Jumpers: Perform actions one and two using hand motions.

Hand Motions
1. Flat hands "on," touching both lengths of rope.
2. Hands over rope and "out."
3. Hands "in" between both lengths of rope.
4. Hands "out."

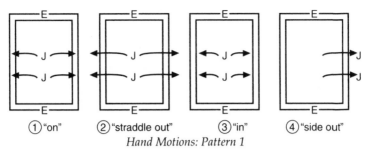

① "on" ② "straddle out" ③ "in" ④ "side out"

Hand Motions: Pattern 1

Hand Motions

1. Using hands, one jumper forms a double diamond in the ropes. The partner joins the jumper in the diamond.
2. The jumpers "spin" three times, holding the diamond shape with their hands.
3. The jumpers jump "out" by travelling under both lengths of rope. The ropes snap back straight.
4. The jumpers stand to the side of the rope. Both put their hands, palm-sides down, over the ropes, touching "on."
5. The jumpers move hands back to "side."

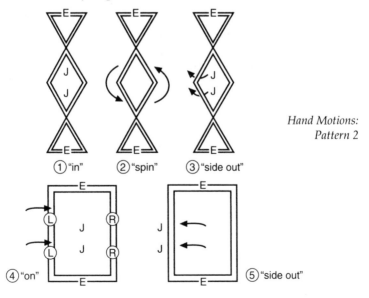

① "in" ② "spin" ③ "side out"

④ "on" ⑤ "side out"

Hand Motions: Pattern 2

Rope Exchange

♦ **Object:** To exchange ropes without a miss.
♦ **Rope Start Position:** Basic
♦ **Number of Players:** 4
♦ **Player Positions**

Basic Position

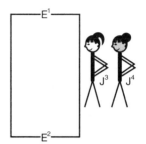

Enders (2): Hold the rope around the ankles in the basic position.
Jumpers (2): Stand facing the rope.

The Game

♦ **Action One**

Jumper 3: Jump "in" the rope. Spread your feet apart.
Ender 1: Jump "out" of the rope. The rope snaps behind jumper 3. The rope is now stretched between ender 2 and jumper 3.

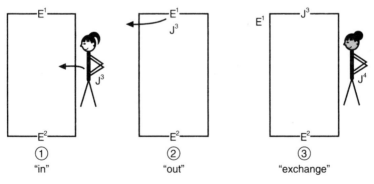

①	②	③
"in"	"out"	"exchange"

♦ **Action Two**

Jumper 4: Jump "in" the rope. Spread your feet apart.
Ender 2: Jump "out." The rope snaps back behind jumper 4. The rope is now stretched between jumper 3 and jumper 4.

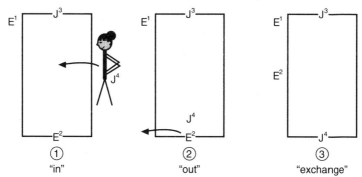

①	②	③
"in"	"out"	"exchange"

♦ **Action Three** Reverse the rope exchange.

Ender 1: Jump "in" the rope. Spread your feet apart.

Jumper 3: Jump "out." The rope snaps back behind ender 1. The rope is now stretched between ender 1 and jumper 4.

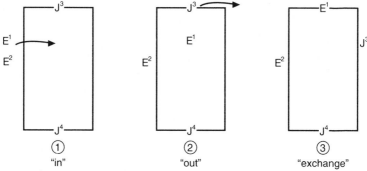

①	②	③
"in"	"out"	"exchange"

♦ **Action Four**

Ender 2: Jump "in" the rope. Spread your feet apart.

Jumper 4: Jump out. The rope snaps back behind jumper 4. The rope is now between ender 1 and ender 2.

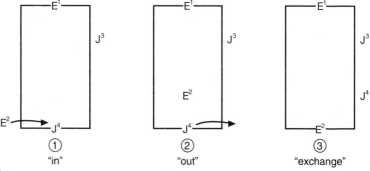

①	②	③
"in"	"out"	"exchange"

84

• **Action Five:** Rope exchange by partners jumping "in" together.

    Jumpers 3 and 4: Jump "in" the rope. Spread your feet apart.

    Enders 1 and 2: Jump "out." The rope snaps back behind and is stretched between jumper 3 and jumper 4.

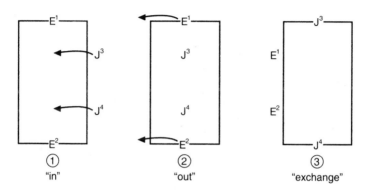

• **Action Six**

    Enders 1 and 2: Jump "in" the rope. Spread your feet apart.

    Jumpers 3 and 4: Jump "out." The rope snaps behind and is stretched between ender 1 and ender 2.

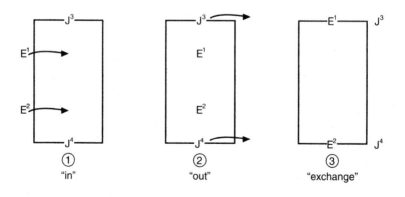

Shapes

- **Object:** To create shapes in the rope.
- **Rope Start Position:** Basic
- **Number of Players:** 5 or more
- **Player Positions**

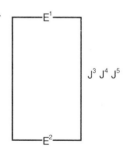

Basic Position

Enders (2): Hold the rope around your ankles in the basic position.

Jumpers (5): Three jumpers wait outside the ropes. Enders 1 and 2 are also active jumpers.

The Game

- **Action One:** Form a triangle

Jumpers: Ender 1: Do not move.

Ender 2: Jump left.

Jumper 3: Jump "in." All jumpers stretch the rope into a triangle.

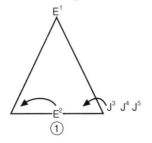 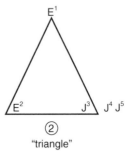

Forming a Triangle

- **Action Two:** Form a square

Jumpers: Ender 1: Jump left.

Ender 2: Do not move.

Jumper 3: Jump forward right.

Jumper 4: Jump "in." All jumpers stretch the rope into a square.

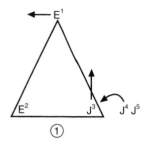
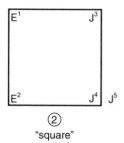

① ② "square"

Forming a Square

♦ **Action Three:** Form a pentagon
Jumpers: Ender 1: Do not move.
Ender 2: Do not move.
Jumper 3: Do not move.
Jumper 4: Jump left middle, then one jump back, forming the pentagon point.
Jumper 5: Jump "in." All jumpers stretch the rope into a pentagon.

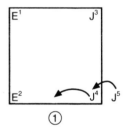
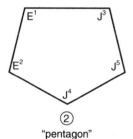

① ② "pentagon"

Forming a Pentagon

Coordination

- ◆ **Object:** To create a sequence of shapes in the rope.
- ◆ **Rope Start Position:** Basic
- ◆ **Number of Players:** 5 or more
- ◆ **Player Positions**

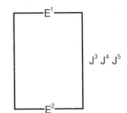

Basic Position

Enders (2): Hold the rope around the ankles in the basic position.

Jumpers (5): Three jumpers wait outside the rope. Enders 1 and 2 are also active jumpers.

The Game

- ◆ **Action One**

Jumpers: Change each shape into the next shape without a mistake. Form the triangle, square, and pentagon in sequence. (See *Shapes* instructions, pages 86–87, for more information.)

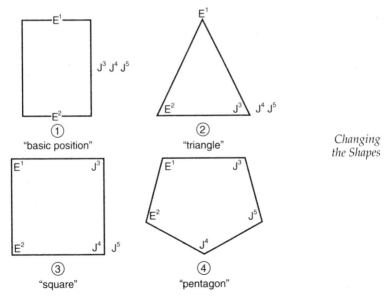

① "basic position"

② "triangle"

③ "square"

④ "pentagon"

Changing the Shapes

♦ Action Two

Jumpers: Reverse the sequence: pentagon, square, triangle, and back to start.

Reversing the sequence:

1. Jumper 4: Jump "out." A square is formed.
2. Jumper 5: Jump "out." A triangle is formed.
3. Jumper 3: Jump "out." Back to basic position.

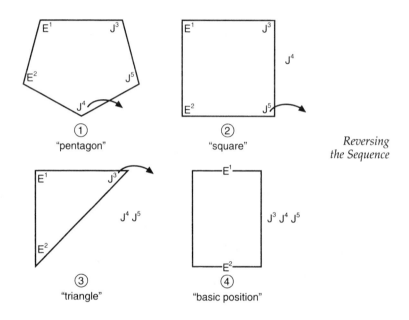

① "pentagon"

② "square"

③ "triangle"

④ "basic position"

Reversing the Sequence

Chinese Rope Kicking

- **Object:** To "karate"-kick the rope forward and backwards without a miss.
- **Rope Start Position:** Modified Basic
- **Number of Players:** 3
- **Player Positions**

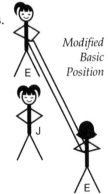

Modified Basic Position

> **Enders (2):** Hold the rope straight and tight with hands at waist height. The Chinese jump rope will look like one rope.
>
> **Jumper (1):** Stand to the side.

The Game

- **Action One**

  Jumper: Touch the rope by kicking, "karate"-kick forward, then "karate"-kick backwards.

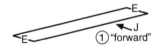

- **Action Two**

  Enders: Raise the rope to shoulder level.

  Jumper: Repeat action one. (As the rope is raised higher, the jumper may move under it for better aim.)

- **Action Three**

  Enders: Raise the rope to neck level.

  Jumper: Repeat action one.

- **Action Four**

  Enders: Raise the rope to head level.

  Jumper: Repeat action one.

- **Action Five**

  Enders: Hold the rope in one fist. Raise the rope by placing the fist on top of the head.

  Jumper: Repeat action one.

- **Action Six**

  Enders: Hold the rope high above the head.

  Jumper: Repeat action one.

Ender Jump

- **Object:** For enders and jumpers to jump patterns actively without a miss.
- **Rope Start Position:** Basic
- **Number of Players:** 3
- **Player Positions**

Basic Position

Enders (2): Enders jump the "ender jump" pattern while holding the rope around the ankles in the basic position.

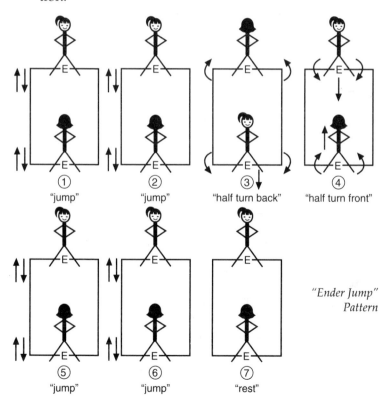

"Ender Jump" Pattern

Jumper (1): Stand sidewards to the rope.

The Game

♦ Action One

Enders: Hold the rope around the ankles. Jump the "ender jump" pattern.

Jumper: Jump Basic Pattern 1.

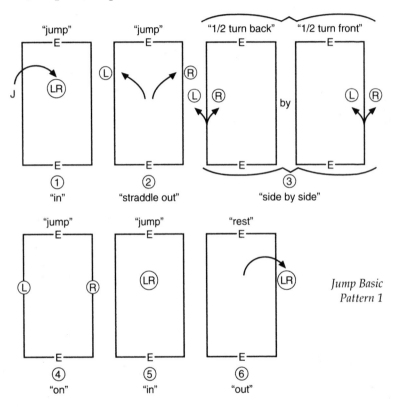

Jump Basic Pattern 1

♦ Action Two

Enders: Raise the ropes. Hold them at knee level. Jump the "ender jump" pattern.

Jumper: Jump Basic Pattern 1.

Tinikling

◆ **Object:** This game is adapted from a Philippine Islands dance, *Tinikling*. Enders and Jumper(s) coordinate rope movements and jumping patterns.

◆ **Rope Start Position:** Modified Basic
◆ **Number of Players:** 3–4
◆ **Player Positions**

Modified Basic Position

Enders **(2):** With your hands, hold the rope in the basic position. Enders will move the rope with their hands, tapping the Tinikling tap pattern.

Jumper(s): Stand sidewards to the rope. A jumper can jump the Tinikling jump pattern alone or with a partner.

The Game

◆ **Action One**

Enders: Begin tapping the Tinikling tap pattern.

1. Tap the rope apart to the play surface for two counts. Call, "Apart 2."
2. Tap the rope together two counts. Call, "Together 2."

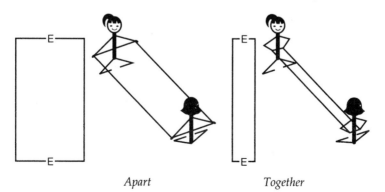

Apart   *Together*

3. Continue the tap pattern until the jumper completes the Tinikling jump pattern.

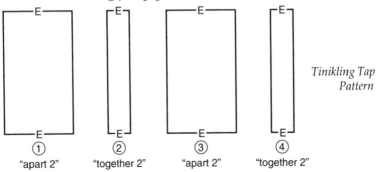

Tinikling Tap Pattern

①	②	③	④
"apart 2"	"together 2"	"apart 2"	"together 2"

♦ **Action Two**

Jumper(s): Jump the Tinikling jump pattern. Prepare to jump right.

Remember: The ropes are moving. Wait until the ropes are *apart* before beginning the jump pattern.

Enders: 1. Tap "Apart 2."

Jumper(s): 2. Jump "in" two counts. Call, "In 2."

Enders: 1. Tap "Together 2."

Jumper(s): 2. Jump "out" two counts. Call, "Out 2."

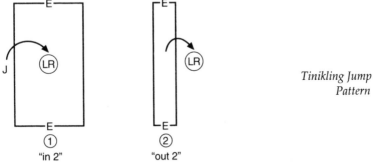

Tinikling Jump Pattern

① "in 2"   ② "out 2"

♦ **Action Three:**

Enders: Continue the Tinikling tap pattern.
Jumper(s): Prepare to jump left.
1. Enders: Apart 2.
2. Jumper(s): In 2.
3. Enders: Together 2.
4. Jumper(s): Out 2.

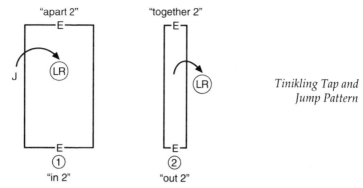

*Tinikling Tap and
Jump Pattern*

♦ **Action Four**

Enders: Continue the Tinikling tap pattern.

Jumper(s): Jump the Tinikling jump pattern four times. One complete pattern is diagrammed.

JUMPING RIGHT:

1. Enders: Apart 2.
2. Jumper(s): In 2.
3. Enders: Together 2.
4. Jumper(s): Out 2.

JUMPING LEFT:

1. Enders: Apart 2.
2. Jumper(s): In 2.
3. Enders: Together 2.
4. Jumper(s): Out 2.

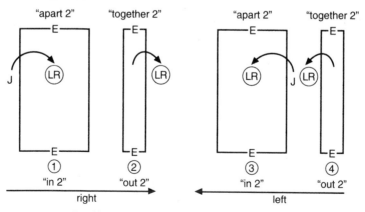

Tinikling Tap and Jump Pattern: Right and Left

Index